A Flutter I

Joanna

Breathe

A Flutter In The Stars

By, Joanna

Poems of Inspiration about Life and Love

Joanna Waechtler

A Flutter In The Stars

There was a flutter in the stars
There is a shift the moment an angel is born
Everything pauses for a brief moment
Almost as if without notice
She is born with purpose
She is born with meaning
She has a destiny, yet a heart of her own
The wind chimes sing
The wolves howl
The rivers flow, the stars shine
The moon gives a smile, knowing
The breeze picks up some leaves
The grass bends
The earth almost shakes
Little does life know
An angel is coming, once again
Little does life know, this time it's different
It's a flutter in the stars
Look close, not just with your eyes but your heart
Maybe then, you'll see

Drive

Drive
Motivation
Stamina
Strength
Dedication
Perseverance
Discipline
Fight
Strength
Hope
Never let go
You're everything

Enter

It is in that moment, that one moment
Between the two worlds
One home to another
A breath of life to a new
Heartbeats quicken
Eyes flutter
Hands reach out and grasp one another
The moment is soft, the new skin fragile
The birds soar, the wolves howl
The moon glistens, and the stars fly
The wind gently blows by
The angels admire
A song is sung
Enter
Enter with wonder
Enter with purpose
Enter with love
It is the one moment between that changes us
One life to the next
One purpose to the next
Enter, sweet child
Welcome, sweet child
Today is your day

On You Go

On you go
Be it your steps
Your smile
Your path
You are the one
And only one
To know yourself
You must rise like a Phoenix
Even if you rise a thousand times
Rise
On you go and will always go
Don't let anything stand in your way
Let them be guides
Not downfalls
Tune in to yourself
You've known all along
On you go
On
You
Go

Fly Free

In all she stands for
How she braved the wind
Stands tall, despite fear
Stands for what she believes in
She honors
She protects
She guides
She's there through it all
Fly, fly
Fly free
Remind them
Guide them home
Bring them peace, love, respect, example
Her colors never fade
She never tires
She never gives up
There is a bigger purpose
Fly
Fly free

Sometimes

Take a breath
Sometimes it helps
When everything rushes by
Nothing is clear
Too many what if's
Don't forget to breathe
Show your beating heart
Pray
Maybe they'll listen
Maybe it's only you
Take a chance? Let it go?
Fight it out, only you will know
A path is ahead of you
But its up to you to pick
It's up to you to choose
Decide which path
Learn, be guided
But the choice is yours
Sometimes it's easy
Sometimes it's hard
Sometimes it's in the hands of angels
Sometimes
It's all in your hands
Take charge
Take the reins
Sometimes, it's all- and only – up to you

Wolves

The clouds part
Everything stands still
There is a silence
The light of the moon shines
Glazing the ground with crystals
Energizing everything in its path
The curious look up in awe
They see its magic, its power
But, one knows it deeper
Knows it more than the moon
One paw forward, one back
Arching neck
Hairs on end
Nails clenched tight
Teeth bared
A deep breath taken, eyes close
A song is sung
Chilling the air
Shuddering the mountains
Cracking the ice
Making fires burn brighter
Nothing is more powerful
More serene
More soulful
More mysterious
Than that of a wolf
And one howling to the moon

Free Spirit

She will not be broken
She will always find her two feet
She knows her worth
She won't stoop down
She guides
She walks her own path
She is wild
She is a free spirit
She will not be broken

Journey

I can't always be there
I wish I could
All I can do is guide
This is your story
Your journey
You will fall
But, you will rise
You'll grow and find strength
You'll cry and you'll laugh
Just know
You have your wings and your heart
Never forget who you are
This is your journey
Ready? Now go, my bird, fly

You

It's not about what you are
Or what you have
It's about who you are
How you treat others
And how you treat yourself

One And Only

Honor yourself
And the space between
Respect yourself
And the faults and successes
Understand yourself
And know it all takes time
Be yourself
And hold strong to the one
And only
You

What If?

What if
You stop
What if
You slow down
What if
You ground
What if
You find yourself
What if
You find your soul
What if?

Queen

A Queen does not falter
Does not fail
She leads and guides
A Queen does not surrender
Does not give up
She knows her worth
A Queen stands tall
Does not fear
She conquers and rises
She is a good Queen
A pure heart, strong
She has good intentions
She is a strong Queen
Leading the path
She helps those on the way
But puts her foot down
And keeps her guard up as needed
She is a Queen

Ashes

It starts slow
It breathes
Moves, devours
It takes everything in its path
No mercy
It has it's own soul
It chokes the air
The creatures flee
Our hearts beat fast
We survive, we stand
Until it's faced with the strong
Who fight back
It meets it's end
Out of the ashes we rise
Out of the fire we are born
It's not easy to get there
But, we do
Ashes may fall
But new life rises
Every
Single
Time

Reason

It's in your blood
Persist. Find a way
You can, and you will
Achieve. Accomplish. Over and over.
Life is worth living
Once you find the reason
You were put here on this earth
For a reason
It's in you. Find it in yourself
Your soul opens
Everything changes
Anything is possible
Put your mind, heart, and soul to it
Never underestimate yourself
Ever

Do You?

What happens when you're lost?

What happens when you're afraid?

Do you hide?

Do you stand tall?

What happens when others judge?

What happens when others disrespect?

Do you hold your ground?

Do you show them your worth?

What happens when you think you've lost?

What happens when you're treated with disrespect?

Do you put them in their place?

Do you show them the right path?

Do you?

Games

I may be good at them
But I won't tolerate the bad ones
I can navigate
But I know where to stop
I can play along
But I won't play for points
I might know how
But I stop here
I stop now
I know me
I know my worth
I don't play those
I don't play those games

Strong

Be strong
If anything
Above all
Despite it all
Be strong

Ripples In Life

A shadow of a dark gloomy day in the unsettling winter's peak

On a mountain high above the tide, above the shores of wonder

She sits and recollects the life she's lived, the life she's known

How vivid it is to her, how cracked the pieces became over time

But, she retraces her footsteps and the winds down the hill

Over the freshly fallen snow, peaks and brush

What was this that life has given to her that nobody else has received?

As her feet guide her down the slopes that soon turn to wet ground

She traces her fingers along her hand

Her hand trembles slightly and she closes her eyes

A wind blows through her hair, and chases her thoughts down to a stream

Where she goes to sit and watch the water flow by, ever so slow

The trees sing in harmony a sweet song she's heard before

A song that was once sung to her when she was young

Don't mistake the past, for she remains at peace, and never forgets

What was and will be always remains

A bird flies by overhead across the sky, and she looks up, smiling

She strokes her hand still, bringing it to her lips

Kisses it and relives her entire life

And how those dreams she's had turned into truth and love

The greatest thing one can receive is love, and be loved

She leans foreward to look at her reflection, seeing herself

She kisses her hand once more, closing her eyes, a tear falls

But what she never believed occurred

She opened her eyes, looked at herself and saw another

She saw the person she always hoped to become

The person she always loved and admired
The person who showed her ripples in her life

A House Of Memory

There is a house I admire, that stands alone

It has a story to tell, and tells it to those who walk by

It has a worn path made of stone, and an old oak tree with a bird
singing a lullaby

It's windows shine in the morning sun, the carpets tearing from
years of tread

The door is cracked open, inviting in all who pass

The pictures on the mantelpiece collect dust over time

All the people in town are on their way to mass, while
Grandfather's clock ticks past

An old rocking chair by the fireplace sleeps, the staircase creaks
from age

A baby's crib is neatly placed where it first learned to crawl

Colors accent a room down the hallway, a bed with a canopy,
overlapping it's dreams

But those cries are silent, no more tears at the seams

Not a sound is heard from the house, not a tone

Just a bird chirping outside the front door

And outside that front door is a porch near that path of stone

Where lemonade was sold, and kids asked for more, where children
played and dogs slept

This house, I'd say, was fairly well kept

But one day, an elderly woman came along as she was singing an
old song

She paused and gathered up her dress, making her way up the path
not making a sound

Opening the door, turning the knob, hearing a creak, she knew
what she was out to seek

She passed by the fireplace, the rocking chair, wishing everyone she
loved was there

But nothing was to be heard, all was quiet, even a bird
She ventured about the house and up the stairs to her room
And noticed all the flowers were suddenly in bloom
The sun came out of the clouds and began to shine
Seeing her crib, she said, "this is mine."
She held her stuffed animal tight, and knew it would be alright
She paused at the photographs, and held them close
She closed her eyes and knew she was home

You

You've taught me about life
And that is all I could ask for
You've show me love and care
And that is what everyone needs
Give me your hand and show me
Which path to take, what road to walk
Guard me; protect me like you say you will
Close your eyes, feel me on your skin
People fight, cry, laugh and smile
But hold on tight, we'll be okay
You've helped me to overcome
The worst things life has to offer
Opening my eyes, I can see it
I see truth, beauty, and love
Time will tell, it's so close
A feeling I've never had before
I now have for you
Tell me you love me; I know you do
I feel it, and I know
That I love you, too

Whisper, Tell Me

It's so loud; don't add to the noise, but now
Just lean over, come close somehow
And whisper into my ear
Tell me your dreams child, my dear
Don't be afraid of the little things
I'll take care of what life brings
Life has balloons, chocolate, and friends
Life has horrors, death, and terrible bends
That twists this way and that
Don't let anyone tell you you're not good enough
Don't let them hurt you
Or I'll come after them too
Now tell me, dear child
Let your dreams go wild

Spirit Of Life

What foul wind is this that is brought upon my soul?

Fret not, dear love, for it will be no more

But oh, 'tis the morning sun, that has found the weakest heart

No more foul winds, no more screams

The river runs free, and the dancers fly high

Soft, is the windowsill that I lay upon

My eyes see so far, but not far enough

I am blinded by the ever changing world

Am I going to scream, or do I need to cover my mouth?

Hear me, hear me; I am the spirit of life within the life

I am the beating heart and the veins under the skin

Does your blood beat so loud? For my ears have gone deaf, no sound

I am entrapped in an engulfing place

I break the horizons and reach to the sky to find that I am alone

What is this? A girl has fallen from the sky

She lays in such a peace, such a grace

What foul wind has brought her here? Shall I lay my hand upon her breast?

Ad bring life back into her?

For I know not of what her life was like

Only that she has fallen and is no more

People cried, they prayed, and sang

Your skin looks so pale and is as cold as the icy walls of hell

What if I awaken her to this life?

And she is nothing more than a foul heart?

Doing nothing but trouble and harming those in her way?

Do you not know who I am?

Do I awaken you, and unwind this endless sleep?
Find the frozen river, break its calm
Find the restless wind, and halt it in it's path
Open your eyes dear child, I found your road
I am in your soul now, don't cry
I am the spirit of life, within the life

What Was, Will Be

There are some things in life that can't change
Many of which go unnoticed
Clouds pass by overhead like a storm over a desert
Yet, all is quiet before the break of a storm
I look behind me and see all that I can see
Is a reflection of you in the falling raindrops
Help me to close my eyes, and calm my hands
Life is coming at me too fast
So, I pray every night that I'll remember
That I'll remember my childhood
And all of the special moments I've had
Time moves on, as do we, but I hope
Our memories don't move on or forget what was
We may not know what will be
And that is a chance we take every day of our lives
But we do know what was
Will be

Staircase Curiosity

I walk down an abandoned hall
And wonder what happened there
I wonder who's lived here and
What they were like
For every person has a gift
Some remain hidden, others not
But what, soft, is this?
A narrow passageway to darkness
I tread with care and wonder
At the bottom are precious things I believe
Photographs and writings lay there
Full of life and secrets for me
To unfold ever so carefully
For if one goes too far
They crumble in their own curiosity
But for one who is careful
They can discover lost memories
And capture a lifetime story
Before a tale is at its end

Change

Some things never change
And I guess neither did you
I didn't intend to tell you what to do
Rather, was just helping you through
Can friendship be lost so fast?
Over something so small, tell me
If you could, would you try once more
Yet maybe if you try, I won't let you
I may not allow you into my life again
Dreams stay dreams, and we live in reality
Can you tell me why you chose to go?
Why you're no longer here to laugh with
You once were my friend, remember?
But I guess some things do change
And a change would do you some good

One Last Thing

The feeling is still here, the presence never leaves, and the denial remains

Time can go no other direction but forward and leaves us lingering behind

The world falls so still and silent when one falls

A feeling came over me, one I could not explain

"Be safe, and don't go too fast," were my last words

If I had known it would be our last, I would have done all I could to spare his life

A shock went through my heart as I grabbed my chest, my heart ached as his heart died

My tears fell, as no more of his tears were shed

My ears screamed and shoved out the truth, too hard to handle

In a little town where I grew up, I never experienced such a silence

Such stillness I could not explain

Checking and double checking didn't bring him back to life again

Looking at him before he entered a permanent state of rest

I screamed and screamed in my head, tears falling down my face

"Breathe, move your chest! Open your eyes, please open your eyes!"

And all was still, nothing moved, nothing was heard, all I could do was stare and wonder

Now all I can do is sit on a patch of grass and wonder what could have been

Wonder what happened, what went through his mind as he died

But nothing, not even tears will bring him back, we all love him, who doesn't?

We all must choose a path when everything begins to close in on us

We can never say for certain what will happen in the end

But all we can do is make the best of the time we have

In times like these, when all lights go out

We must remember the beauty of life, how soft, precious, and fragile it is

To lose it in an instant, and never know, the choices we make can affect our lives

What must we do to bring back the past?

All we can do is remember and learn, carry our knowledge

And pass it to further minds, what we do in life echoes an eternity

If I could say one last thing, it would be, "be careful, everyone loves you."

Soldier

I sat upon my chair on a starlit night
Nothing to do but listen to the thunder in the night
But in the mist not far from my eye appeared a man
But, once closer, a soldier
"Excuse me, miss, please help me,
I am cold and have seen it all
I saw her die without notice
Without pain,
She sings a song in heaven now.
I am covered in dirt and blood."
He pleaded and held his hand close to his heart.
He fought, he killed, he suffered
"I've seen too much," he continued,
"I have seen death, screams, children
All fallen apart
But you, whom I know
To have a kind soul. Let me in, feed me
Don't leave me stranded in this ghostly place."
His eyes gleamed.
He tilted his head and looked at the floor
I reached out my hand and took him in
Fed him, clothed him
And gave to him
A life like none other
And I fought with mine to save his

Push On

She does not tire
She does not break
She pushes on, finds a way
She knows her own heart
She breathes in deeply
The wind blows through her hair
Her heart flutters as she looks up
She looks up knowingly
She is changed, she is set
She knows her path
She knows her worth
She knows her fight
So, she stands and pushes on

Kingdom

You are a kingdom
Your mind, body, soul
Treat it as such
Even when nobody is looking

Friends

They stand by your side
They give words with care
Sometimes sweet, fun words
Sometimes firm, but true words
They have your back
They do not falter
They are there through it all
Whether they are in your presence
Or far away
Distance does not separate a friendship
For friends remain tied, bonded
Small circles are worth having
They know you the best
And they know what's best for you

Life

It's all a journey
We must live
We must face
People come
And people go
But everything
Leads to…
The story of our lives
Some we expect
And dream for
Some
We never saw coming
Everything plays a role
Everything has a voice
Tune in
Look up
Pay attention
You only get this once
And everything
Every moment
Matters

You Know

You know who your true friends are
You find out who your "friends" were
You see who was just there
You understand yourself
You have the small circle
Rid yourself of the fakes
The spies, the lies
The untrue
You know who

Moments

Slow

Still

Breathe

Close your eyes

It's in these moments

You'll see

Stop

Forget everything else

This is what you've been missing

The Beauty Of A Woman

The beauty of a woman
The beauty of women
The beauty of a tribe
Women are all as one and are the most
Mystical, magical, powerful
Beings on this planet
We have a fire in our soul
With angel wings on our backs
We have thick skins and understanding
Forgiving hearts
But our blood is made of steel
We thrive together
We survive together
The power lies within lifting one another up
Supporting each other
Fighting for and alongside each other
We are so different on the appearance end
But are so similar deep within
Embrace your woman
Embrace your tribe
Embrace you

Dawn

It was quiet, calm, dark
Mist lined the roads and hills
The moon was shining brightly, reflecting
The stars were breathtaking
There was a feeling in the air
She took in a deep breath
She looked around, observed quietly
The lanterns lit up, ignited
She stopped. She felt something
There was an energy behind her
A tree that bend up and curved to the right
She looked back at the lanterns
Still feeling something
Her soul ignited, all of the colors
Reds, blues, pinks, greens, purples
The lanterns held their light, twinkling
Igniting
As her soul ignited, like a flame
It was magic, she was glowing
All of her colors, all that she was
She breathed in, breathed out
One crisp, cold
Magical, beautiful morning

Electric

She went back and forth
Should she go? Should she stay?
There was a pull she couldn't ignore
She decided, she went
It's as if it was known she'd be there
A force, an energy to be reckoned with
There was excitement, like butterflies
The air seemed to dance like lightning
Everything felt on fire
All eyes were on her, but she was focused
As if everyone disappeared
Her heart pounding, adrenaline rushing
Her eyes surged, taking it all in
It felt like an earthquake
But nobody moved
Everything was electrified
It took her breath away
Knocked her to her knees
The ultimate power
The ultimate energy
It could be felt for miles
It was in that moment, she knew
Everything became clear
Her soul ignited

Example

It's okay to stand out
To be different, unique
Be looked at
You'll be judged, questioned
Many won't know or understand
But you'll also be admired
Respected
Looked up to
You will inspire others
By those who say it
And more by those who don't
Keep it up
Keep being you

Conquer

Conquer
Fall
Conquer
Fall
Without falling
From the challenges life has
You'd never learn how to rise
Without gaining strength
From the ups and downs
You wouldn't be who you are today
Conquer
Fall
And conquer

Mother

There is nothing stronger
Than a mother
Who pours her heart out
For her little beating hearts
There is no bigger protector
Than a mother
Who would do anything
For her little souls
There is nothing more giving
Than a mother
Who may not always be perfect, but does her best
For her little people
There is nothing stronger
Than a mother's love
For her children

Lost

I know you feel lost
You may feel small, defeated
You're reading this to find answers
Or something to relate to
Or words to speak what's in your heart
I see you. I know and I understand
Keep your chin up, stand tall
Protect your heart
Answers will come, things will work out
Take my hand, I'll show you the paths
You must decide, but I'll guide
I'll walk beside
Keep going, you're strong
Never forget that
I believe in you
I see you
I know

Forgive Yourself

It's something you'll never forget
Only some will understand
Little do they know
Whether it's said in silence
Or screamed out loud
The memories will always be there
The nightmares
The questions, emotions
Even when the fog and fear begin to clear
It's always there
You can and will rise, become strong
Fight on
Promise me this
Forgive yourself
Love and respect yourself
I see you
I understand
I hold you in my heart
And give you my strength
You're not alone
Don't forget who you are
Forgive yourself
I am with you
You got this
Take my hand
Let's fly

Push On

Keep pushing on
To get
To where you want to be

The Man At The Table

What's next? The man sat there, slowly finishing his food. His eyes glancing at the empty chair across from him. He has stories to tell, and nobody to tell them to.

He pictured his love sitting across from him. He learned to tune out the bad, soak in the mood. But, his heart ached. He was a peaceful, gentle man who frequently relived memories. He had one less worry tonight.

When the waitress came, the bill was paid. Someone saw him. Someone noticed him. A small act touched his heart. He left with a smile on his face knowing an angel was watching him.

Smile

Keep smiling…right?

What do you say when you break down and cry?

When nobody's looking?

They only see you smile

So they think you're a phony and a fake

That you make things up or exaggerate

Or try to get attention

That's far from the truth

Stop. Pay attention.

Like how not all disabilities are visible –

Not all smiles mean everything is okay

Or that someone is happy.

Be careful what you think

Before you actually know

By asking the source

I

I
Don't
Forgive
You.
I never will.

But.

I forgive
Myself.

What If? And?

What if
What if it was different
What if you never left
It's like a book
Where you choose your fate
And flip to that page
Anything can change in an instant
There's room for change
But some things can never be forgiven
Some things are meant to be
Maybe one day we'll meet
Amongst the stars

Circle

Truths told and untold
Judged, unknown
No inquiries, no desire
But based off lies and outsiders
You know nothing
You don't care to know
It's okay
You're not part of my circle
My small circle
Keep it small
Look no further
Your best, and trusted are there
They know
They care

It's Okay

It's okay to cry
It's okay to scream
You feel lonely
Hurt
Betrayed
Lost
Mad
Confused
Everything
I understand
Let's get it out
Cry it out
Tomorrow is coming
We got this

Two Way

So simple
So profound
Will you give back
What I pour in?

It's a two-way street
If we don't meet there
I'll say goodbye here

Words

Sometimes
The strongest words
Are those –
That are not said at all

Are You Okay?

And who is there when you scream?
When you cry?
When you fall?
And who is there to have your back?
To guide you?
To give you strength?
And who is there to reach out
And ask –
Are you okay?

Anyone?

Anyone?

Look

Look
There
Yes, there
Deep down
At the core of it all
You have the answers
You know
Now, take it and fly

Forgive Yourself

Forgive
Forgive yourself

Oh, this isn't for you
But – it's about you
Demons don't swim
In Angel waters
This isn't for you
Oh, hah, no

This is for me
This if for those like me
Who have been there
And those who are there
I speak to, for, and with you

This is a letter
A forgiveness for myself
From what you did
And who I am

I forgive myself
I free myself
You are not a part of me
You are not my fear
Only a distant memory
That made me stronger

To avoid those like you
Now, I know, even better
I know the truth
That's all that matters
I know myself
That's all that matters
I am even stronger
I forgive myself
I love myself
I accept myself

I forgive
Myself

Wild And Free

Want my heart?
Keep me free
Want my love?
Keep me free
Leave me be
Free and wild
As I am
As I was born
And meant to be
I can't, and won't be tamed
I am not yours, or anybody's
I am me
Myself
My own
Respect it
Leave it be
Honor it
Set me free
Because at heart and in spirit
I am wild and free

Life

We are all in this together
We need to be honest with ourselves
Be kind, helpful
Be passionate, driven
Be strong, be courageous
Be empathetic
It's a journey
Of adventure, excitement
Learning, empowerment
Triumph and defeat
We rise and fall
Our journey is our own
But we are on this with everyone
Why not help each other?
Guide, be there?
It's not a competition
Not a fight
We should encourage
This is life
An amazing adventure we have
In the palm of our hands
In our heart, mind, body, and soul
This is life
We are all in this together

Journey

We only live this life once
So, live it to the fullest
And enjoy every moment
But, what does that truly mean?
Deep within the outer shell
It sometimes takes an awakening
To see
To deeply understand
It's a journey
And we do only live this life once
It's how we learn, cope, change
It's how we challenge, grow, come to
Every step takes us somewhere new
Somewhere unexpected
There will be many "aha!" moments
But when you have THOSE few
You'll know
And it will change everything
For the better

Curves

Every curve, mark, scar
Every bump, rise, and fall
Has a story to tell
It traces far beyond galaxies
To the depths of the universe
Her body was so vast
Complex and unknown
Her veins pulsed with her energy
That could not be caught
Her heart surged with a force
That could not be reckoned with
Her soul wildly and fiercely danced
It would never be understood
Her eyes were the key
The rest told a story
Every curve
It's what's beneath it all
Through the key
You'll find, and see
Who she really is

Sign

I'm waiting
I'm waiting for a sign
You can only find it
When you aren't looking
But don't miss it
It's exactly what you're looking for
Trust the process
Listen to your soul
Know yourself
Wait and see
You'll find it

Words

What words are there
When the tongue runs dry
And the mind, slow
When they used to flow
They pause, they wait
For they should not be forced
Even the mind needs time
As the heart and soul
Needs breaks and grounding
It'll come my dear, it will
It's in the right time
And the right moment
That the words will run clear
And flow with power and purpose
Trust

Crash

Breathe
Take it slow
Crash
Thrown
Tossed
Slam
Like a whip back and forth
Darkness
Open your eyes
There you are
Haze
Pain like fire
Breathe
Fear
Anger
Confusion
Questions
Time
Denial
Cycle
Pain
Ever changed
Not the same
Crash
Open your eyes
Dream again
You will

Rise again

Angel

Guardian

Wings

You'll be okay

In time

Ophelia

Ophelia, oh, Ophelia
So soft
So delicate
A bird would land on your shoulder
Sing songs unsung
The things you see, you do
Nothing but a kind heart
But one driven mad by love
Mad by the world around you
Surrounded by the stream
The birds, the lilies
The bouquet of flowers
So still, you lay
So troubled, yet so peaceful
Did she find her home here
At her resting place?
Maybe only the birds will know
Ophelia, oh, Ophelia

Balance, Between

Those few seconds
Between needing air
And enjoying the quiet
Between taking a breath
And enjoying the view
Before coming up out of the water
Or looking down the lane
Both so beautiful
Each choice important
Find the balance
The balance between
The two worlds
The two decisions
The two experiences
You'll need some of both
To know how to swim

River

It flows so gently
It runs so deep
It comes and it goes
The places it sees, it touches
I envy it
It's wild and free
Calm and churning
It explores and it rests
In and out with the tides
Following the heart of the moon
It has it's own beating heart
A free spirit
Maybe that's why I feel so at home
When I'm around the water
Wild and free
Beat of my own drum
Dancing with the moon
Running with the deer
Singing with the birds
Feeling the energy between my fingers
As it flows telling it's story
Stop. Pause. Breathe
You'll find yourself there
With what makes your soul ignite

Beating Heart

The heart is intricate
Balanced
Powerful, supplying
It holds scars, trying to repair
But some remain
It continues to beat
Deliver everywhere important
But fool me twice
The heart won't recover from that
The scar remains
But it is a strong scar
And one that knows now
How to avoid such a break
Your heart, like you
Cannot learn, grow, be strong
Without having encountered
And gained some scars along the way
Keep beating, my heart
But, fool me again, those doors will close
For what's inside
Is much stronger
Than before

Wings

Give a woman her wild freedom
And she'll never forget she has wings

Give a woman pain, tears, and heartache
And you'll see the power of those wings

Set Her Free

What if —
While I was being deceived
She found her footing
What if —
While I thought I knew
She grew her wings
What if —
While I was violated
She learned to fly
What if —
While when I was hurt
She became free
What if —
While I suffered
I set her free?

One Moment

A chance, a moment
A flutter, a racing heart
It's unexpected, like the cracking smile
The blush, the peace
Who knew? Life works in magical ways
A simple word, an entire meaning
A flow like a wave in the ocean
A peaceful blue, a song dolphins dance to
A connection, a reason
A setting sun kissing the horizon, a flash
A curiosity, a wonder
A sprinkle of stardust across the sky
All in a chance, a moment

Daisy

The daisy petals will tell
Loves me, loves me not?
Keep me, betray me?
Find luck, find loss?
Be strong, be weak?
Trust, broken trust?
Confident steps, wavering?
Knowledge, a closed mind?
Stay, go?
This or that?
What if?
We always ask
The daisy petals will tell
It's up to us to decide
Find and walk our own path
In the end

S.O.S.

I hear your whisper
I see your poker face
All the tears you tried to hide
All the fights you had to endure
I hear your cries
I see your broken heart
All the aching you have inside
All the smiles you try to fake
I hear your spirit
I see your fight, ready to rise
I hear you, it's been there all along
I see you, I know you
I got your S.O.S.
Take your whisper and scream
Take your tears and run
I know the fights
Now it's your turn to fly
Your guardian angel is always there
Showing you the way
S.O. S.
It's your turn to fly
Fly

Wild Souls

Run with the wild souls
Admire them, observe them
Respect them, they respect back
But don't catch them, trap them
Don't betray their trust
They have wild wings
Hidden away, to be used
And they'll never look back

Be

In an ever-changing world
Be kind
In a time of confusion
Be present
Look up at the things around you
See the people
Notice the colors
Feel the energies
Sense the feelings
Breathe in the wind
Hear the pulse of the living things
Be the look in someone's eye
That makes their day
A little thing can have a big impact
Maybe more than you could ever imagine
In an ever-changing world
Be kind
Be there

A Feeling

It starts with a feeling
And when society tells you
What to think
How to feel
How to go about things
Deep down you differ
A little bit of me was left behind
Waiting to be found
I had to follow the trail
And pick up the pieces
Steps forward
Steps backwards
It was a feeling I had
A feeling I lost
A feeling I regained
I know how to feel
I know how to think
I forgive myself
I found my pieces
I feel alive
I feel strong
I feel home
I feel like
ME

Soul On Fire

Don't play with fire
They say
Run away from it
They say
Put it out
They say
My darling, you are the fire
Be the fire, breathe the fire
You can rage and tear through
Unstoppable, nothing stands in your way
Yet, along the way, you give new life
New meaning, new purpose
Hope, rebuilding
Ignite your soul
Do what sets your soul on fire
And keep that flame lit
In the darkest of times
And the best of times
Use it to light the way for others
With great power, there are choices
Responsibilities
Use it wisely
Never forget who and what you are
And that your soul is made of fire

Sober

It's done, time to move on
Never look back
You make mistakes
Things happen
They knock you off your feet
But they do not define you
They're all part of the journey
It's what we do with the knowledge
Of ourselves and what we learned
Where we will find the keys to life
It takes discipline and strength
Determination and will
To rise after a fall
When you overcome depression, darkness
Overcome trauma, emotional and physical
Overcome toxins you put into your body
Overcome health issues
Everything you overcome, big or small
You win
You're sober and clean
Now rise
Show others their keys
Be their guide and inspiration
To a sober, happy life

Body, Soul

My body is my temple
My soul is my universe
And I will treat it as such
Learn to forgive yourself
Put the effort in
That which is worth having
Won't be easy
It cannot be done
By anyone but ourselves
The paths twist and turn
Fork and dead end
Find yours, make the choices
You have this life once
Make it worth it
Accept and know who you are
Wear your scars with confidence
Cry, but wipe the tears away
Stand tall, find your ground
Feel your heart beat
In every situation
You'll find your wings
Respect yourself first
Love yourself first
Be there for you
Your body is a temple
Your soul is the universe

Surreal

It's indescribable
It took just one look
To give me a thousand smiles
That feeling I get
It's like a rush
Like a raging river
Yet as calm as a glass lake
It's peaceful
It's real
The comfort I have
Knowing you understand
See things differently
Keep me safe
But keep me free
It's surreal
And it's indescribable
How real it actually is

Crumble

When lines are crossed
Boundaries pushed
Mistakes, frequent
Questions come to light
Pick a flower
Pull the petals
See where it ends up
Fool her once
She forgives
Fool her twice
It crumbles
Too many pieces to rebuild
Too much flown away in the wind
Like a distant memory
She runs with wolves
She won't be chased by them
For if she is
She will lead she pack
Never underestimate a wild woman
Paths to her may crumble along the way
But her wings will never falter
Every time brings new growth
Bigger, fuller wings
To take flight
When the strong path is found
For that which is meant to be

Simple

It's a simple thing
To respect a woman
To treat her well
To love her right
But it' s a two-way street
She will pour out her heart
And every effort
But should the street
Merge into one
She'll gladly take the road
That goes off the path
She'll find her own
She always will
Women
Are simple beings
Fierce, strong, capable
But never to be crossed
Or taken for granted

The Small Things

The rock skips across the surface
Followed by laughter
As a bird flutters by
Curious eyes trail it's path
A deer raises it's head, pausing
It is being watched with wonder
A rainbow appears after the rain
Creating sparkles in hearts
The soft fur moves like grass in the wind
Sending tingles down spines
The small things, taken for granted
Are noticed, appreciated and adored
By those with the biggest hearts
The most adventurous minds
And of absolute imagination
They are children
Small things
It's the small things

Go

Feel that?
Feel that push?
Stop resisting it
Take that step
Don't hold back
Take a deep breath
And go

Not Worthless

You're not worthless
I'll stop you from saying those words
Please look up
It's me
I give you my truth
A truth as others also see in you
You are strong
Please never give up
Never give in
These tears that fall from your face
Will soon fade
You are cared for
Admired, loved
You are not worthless
Let those words leave your tongue
Please look up
It's you that's worth fighting for

Empty

Empty words
Empty actions
Empty promises
You, empty
What seemed to be
A long-lasting love
Soon revealed otherwise
When she poured out her everything
To get emotional wounds
Doubt, frustration
To find it was a one-way street
Empty everything's
She didn't go crazy
No, she protected her heart
She grew
She found her true self
Instead of pouring into emptiness
She poured it into herself
Was she crazy for putting herself first
After pouring into emptiness?
I think not
She is bolder, stronger
Aware, she knows her worth
She'll never break to play that game
She knows the rules
She'll make her own
And she'll continue to grow

And love herself fully
Never to be empty or treated as such
Ever again

You Should

You should
You really should care
Care about yourself
Stop caring about what others think
Of course it'll hurt
I'm not saying it won't at times
But, remember who you are
You should
When you get lost, find yourself again
Because you should
Stop giving a (oh yes, you know what)
About what others think
You should put yourself first
Care about what you say to yourself
And
You should care about yourself

Responsibility

As a human, you have a responsibility

As a male, female

As a mother, father

As a daughter, a son

As a sister, brother

As a cousin

As an animal owner

As anything and everything

You have responsibilities

You can't let others do for you

You need to take action

You need to do and be

We are all in this together

But we each individually

Must be responsible

Take responsibility

Own it

Find Me

You'll find me there
Amongst the willows and the streams
In the depths, riding the waves
Catching the sunsets, watching the sunrises
Chasing the moon
Running with the wind
Dreaming with the stars
Frolicking with the horses, soaring with eagles
Cuddling with sparrows, swimming with whales
Watching the wolves, crawling with hunting lions
Embrace the power around me
Honoring the energy
Holding what is true
Knowing what is there, with everything
There –
You'll find me

Coma

A place between
Your own breath
And that which is given to you
Resting, healing
Fighting, hoping
Dreaming, soaring
Let your body heal
Let your mind rest
Promise me this
That you'll wake
Open your eyes to another day
Remember who you are
And continue the fight
Even after the machines are done
This life is worth living
And it needs your smile
And kind heart in it
Keep healing
Keep breathing
Keep fighting
Please, when it's time
Wake up
We love you

Serendipity

You can hope, dream
Try to find
Look, and look
But, it's when you don't try
That things happen
Come your way
By chance
Like magic
Was it meant to be?
Coincidence?
We may never know
The only word
To describe this magic is
Serendipity

Smile

She smiled
Because
It was the small things
That he did for her
That meant everything
It made her heart sing
It reminded her
She was cared for, respected
So, she smiled
And in return
She gave her heart, her all
It's simple
To make her smile
It's just as simple to do the opposite
And lose it all
A woman knows
Her boundaries
What she wants and needs
What makes a man
What love is
When to stay, when to work
When to leave, spread her wings
It's a two-way street
Smile
It's simple, for some
Smile

Woman

The best thing a woman can wear
Is a smile
But not one across her lips
One that shines
From her eyes
Glowing from her soul
Yes, that is a beautiful woman

Tune Back In

You're spinning
Slow it down
You're running
Catch your breath
You're lost
Follow the trail
You're focus is dimming
Ground your soul
You're darting
Calm your heart
We lose ourselves
Time to time
Stop
Tune back in
You'll find yourself again

Hush, Hush

Do you hear that?

Hush, hush

Listen, not with your ears

With your inner being

It sings songs of generations

Stories told around fires

Epic sunrises and sunsets

Every breath, every beating heart

Surges of adrenaline

Rises of endorphins

Memories

Love

Life

Do you hear that?

Deep within?

It exists within you

You'll find it, see it

You'll hear it

Hush, hush

Process

They say take it day by day
Moment by moment
Breathe in
Exhale
Sometimes things play out
What's meant to be
When it's meant to happen
Trust the process
Trust yourself
There will always be a lot
Always
All you can do
Is one by one
Day by day
Moment by moment
And it will always
When it's right
Fall into place

Webs

We all create webs
Webs of life
Deep within our webs of truth
We also create webs of lies
Webs of hope
Webs of defeat
Webs of success and more
Spinning, designing
Taking apart, recreating
Intricate designs
Each serving a purpose
How big, how small
How detailed, how fine tuned
How it's placed, how it's held
How it's stitched together
How it's rebuilt after collapse
We all create webs

Notice

Do you ever notice
The person staring off
Someone feeling down
Someone hiding their feelings
With a poker face
Do you ever ask
If someone is okay
If they need to talk
How they, genuinely, are
If they need help
Do you ever see
The person being strong
The person trying to find
The person who needs a friend
The person who...
Well...
Do you?
Do you notice?

The Voice

There's a voice when I call
At the other end of the line
The calm they have
While tears run down my face

There's a voice when I answer
At the other end of the line
The panic they have
While I get them the help they need

There's a voice and lights
At the front door knocking
The determination they have
To help

There's a voice and tears
At the front door, unlocking
The look of hope they have
As help arrives

We are all in this together
We call when we need help
They answer the line
They show up, help
Serve, protect
The voice

Messengers

We've all heard of being touched by an angel
Having guardian angels
Messages from heaven
That we're being watched over, protected
It's true what they say
Angels, and those dear to our hearts, that have passed
Live amongst us still
They come in many forms
The breeze blowing in the wind through our hair
A memory suddenly appearing in our minds
The feeling that someone is there
A bird, a sparrow nearby
Feathers dancing all around, making appearances
Dragonflies, shimmering like rainbows
Unexplained happenings
It's them
They're there
The messengers, guardians, angels, loved ones
You're not alone

Touch

A quiver, sensations

Goosebumps down the arms

Tingles up the spine

Hearts racing in rhythm

Eyes rolling, hair pulling

Hands clenching

Sweat dripping

Sounds of electricity

It's in the touch

It's in the connection

It's what's real

That's what makes it come alive

The Quiet Ones

The loud presences in the room
Don't always mean power
Or confidence
Never underestimate the quiet ones
You mistake them for being shy
For lacking
But trust me
They're listening, watching
Absorbing, observing
They're the ones who have the louder presence
They have the power
Oftentimes by being quiet
More is said with the eyes
And more is understood
By listening, watching
They're often mistaken
But make no mistake
About the quiet ones

Not Alone

I see your heart on the floor
I also see you sweep it under the rug
I see the fight in your eyes
I see your good days and I also see your pain
Trust me, I've been there too
So, when I see it, no matter how good of a poker face
I know
I see you
You're not alone

Times

There were times for holding back
There were times for holding on
There were times for poker faces
There were times for tears
There were times for wondering, wishing
There were times for letting go
There were times for putting your foot down
There were times for holding your ground
There were times for doing
There were times for taking action
There were times for spreading wings to fly
There were times to make a change
There were times to conquer
There were times for smiles and laughter
There were times for confidence
There were times to know and be yourself
There were times to take that step forward
There were times to make that change
There were times to trust the process
There were times to trust yourself
What will your time be?

Do For You

Let yourself be happy
Set yourself free
Don't change for others
Change for yourself
Break those chains
Spread those wings
Dig deep
Go down a different path
Don't hold back
Try new things
Challenge yourself
Do this for YOU
There you'll find
Your growth
Your change
Your adventures
Your voice
Your confidence
What you were looking for
What you were needing
YOU

Lighting The Way

She dances fearlessly
She aims, she fights
With the strength from her Greek blood
She walks as light as a feather
And makes her presence known when needed
She carries with her ancient wisdom
Knowing the ways, trusting forces around her
The strong women living in her veins
She sees them dance in the firelight, fearlessly
They reach for the stars, to light the way
She is
A goddess
A warrior
A soul on fire
She is
A woman

I Guess

I guess things happen
When they're meant to
Or not
I guess it's meant to be
Or maybe it's not
I guess friends come and go
Even the best ones
You think would be forever
I guess love comes and goes
We all know that tale
I guess dreams rise and fall
Like the air we breathe each day
Like our hearts
Pounding away
I guess this life is worth living
Until it says goodbye
I guess this fight, purpose, drive
Has a reason, or maybe not
Maybe another is meant to be
I guess that's just life
No matter what it is
It comes, goes
Meant to be, or not
I guess
But we'll never know
Unless we try

Like Flying

The only love
Is one of trust
Of presence and effort
Free of jealousy and control
Free of monitoring and pain
Love is like breathing
Like flying
For those that find it
It is like magic
Hold on to it
We go through trials
Some teach lessons
Some painful, some great
Some are bridges
Some never meant to be
That end up in the dust behind
Or last as a friendship
And they say
You'll know when you see it
Feel it. Find it
You'll know
Why?
It's like flying

Treat Her

Treat her with respect
Trust. Honesty
Leave her be
Let her be free
Like a goddess
Like a fragile bird
Like a strong mountain
Like a fierce lion
Like a graceful mustang
Full of soul
Power. Grace
Beauty. Spirit
Treat her as such
And she'll give her all
Treat her without
And she'll give it all up

Running

Many choices and things
Will break your heart
But nothing
Will break your soul
What have you been running from
All this time
Toward and away from
It's time to stop
Catch your breath
Stand up tall
Claim who you are
No more running
This is your show now
Take all you've learned
All you've seen, been through
Give me that wink
Now go
Don't run. Fly

As It Should Be

Free and strong
Wild and ignited
Fierce and loving
Passionate and graceful
Is the woman
Who has no cage
Who makes the choice to fly
As it should be

Little Voice

I used to wonder where I went wrong
What path I should've taken
What I should've said, or maybe not said at all
I drive myself crazy into sadness, despair
Hurt, anger, confusion
I was lost looking up from a long dark tunnel
Until
A little voice, who was there all along
Screaming at me finally caught my attention
This voice knew all along, I failed to see
I forgave myself and decided to rise
I didn't want this, this wasn't me
So, I listened. I changed. I tried
Even in trying, I succeeded and failed
But I grew stronger instead of going down the dark tunnel
My soul sparked, ignited
My eyes became clear
My mind free, my body strong
A sense of being and who I am
Who I was meant to be
I know where I went wrong, I change it
I choose the right paths now
Even if I stray, I find my way back
I say what I mean and when I need to
I drive myself crazy into happiness, discovery
Strength, hope, growth, love
I was lost but am no longer

Because I listened to my voice
I had ignored too long
Because of that voice
I listened
I thrive
You can, too

Meant To

When
It's meant to

How
It needs to

Why
It needs to

When and Where
It needs to

Patience

Care Or Not

Just because I hear you
When you're loud
Or even when you're silent
Doesn't mean I have to join in
It doesn't mean I have to care
Or put my energy and effort
In to a roundabout repeat
I can care, most the time I do
That's who I am
Unless you forgot
Or can't accept it
So, I care

Boundaries

Don't like me? Who I am?

What I stand for?
How I grow? How I change?

How I become a better version of myself?

And not just for me – for my kids?

Get out of my way.

Oh. Please. And thank you.

I have my own healing to do

My own health to deal with

My own things to figure out

My own goals to smash and achieve

Above all, I have

My children. They're my everything

I have myself. I am my everything

I have to be the best me, to be the best mom, to be the best for my
kids

This is my journey

My process

My boundaries

Respect it.

Or leave.

Oh. Please. And thank you.

Never

You never think it'll be you
Until it is
You'll deny it
Until you know it's true

Only then, can you heal and change

Other End Of The Line

To the heroes
Behind the line
Who answer the call
The Thin Gold Line
Tirelessly
They're there
Night and day
During the worst times
To be the voice
At the other end of the line

Answer

"Tell me something I need to know," I said to my child

He looked at me. Paused, in thought.

He put his hands over my eyes.

I smiled.

He lay his head on my heart.

It was then.

I knew. I found my answer.

Here For You

I hear you
When you're silent
I see you
When you cry
I know
When you poker face
I'm here for you
I see you
Trust me
I do

Okay

Nope
I'm not okay
Right now
But
I'll be okay
And that's
Okay

My Own

No more will I do
To please you
To keep you comfortable
To fit in
To worry
It's mine
My own
Me
I will do for me
I will sing my own songs
Dance under the stars
Do what makes me smile
What makes my heart fly
It's my life
My decisions
What I do is not up to you
My happiness is mine
My own

Pain

Smiling through it all
Nobody would even know
What's firing off within
What will always remain
I'm tired of this pain

Healthy

Be free
Be you
Choose
No worries
No boundaries
No control
Just trust
Love
Freedom
Understanding
Support
To be
That is
What healthy relationships
And friendships
And care of self
Are made of

Fear

Nothing has stopped me yet
I've seen the devil's share
Thrown at me from outside and within
My heart and my mind are strong
My shield thick
My soul won't cave
Try me
Feel the power of these wings
Cause they won't stop
Fear her, watch your back
When she looks fear
And fire
In the face
And smiles
See the power
Of those wings

Demons

We all have inner demons
No matter what the battle
I hear your prayer, your plea
I see your fight, your pain
I'm here, everything's okay
We'll figure out a way
To make the demons
Go away

Until It's You

You'll never know
Until it's you
The songs, words
Meanings
The way things feel
How things change
You'll never know
Someone else's story
Or what it means
Until it's you

True Beauty

True Beauty
Within a woman
Comes from her heart
Her soul, her being
But above all
Her True Beauty
Comes from
Her genuine smile
That is the best thing
A woman can wear

Heart

What does your heart beat for

It pulses strongly

When you wake

And as you sleep

What does your heart fight for

As you breathe in

All life has to offer

The good, the bad

The hardships

The successes

If you're lost

You'll find yourself here

If you're in pain

Physically, emotionally

You'll find yourself here

In your heart

Don't forget it

Say

I may say a lot
Share a lot
But there's much
You don't know
You'll never understand
Whether I say or not
So, don't be so quick
To judge or assume
About what I say
Or what's not said at all

No

Oh, no
No, no, no

No.

You don't have that kind of power
Not over her.
Ever.

Who You Are

I see you
I know you
I understand
I see you
As you are
Who you've been
Who you are
And what you want to be
And
I love you
For who you are

Fading

I can't breathe
I can't keep my head above water
I'm drowning
I can't think
I can't keep my mind from wandering
I'm suffocating
I can't see
I can't keep my eyes from tearing
I'm faltering
I can't be
I can't keep my soul from escaping
I'm fading

Look Up

Pay attention
Look up and you'll see
All the small things
That are now missed
The details
The things between the lines
That show and tell us
Who we are all meant to be
Look up
And you'll see

Quiet

We can share our thoughts
Or hide them
We can scream them
Whisper them
Some need to be shared
Some better left unsaid
Sometimes the best ones
Are quiet
In a special place
A place where they can be kept
Thought on, felt
No judgement, no ears
Except our own
Our mind is a safe place
But not to be taken for granted
Too many and it'll shatter
Use it to keep some thoughts safe
Share the rest
Because in this place
It's safe
It's quiet

Deepest Tears

The deepest tears
From the deepest feelings
Come only at night
When they can't be seen
Or explained
Other than your own heart

Pillow

Your pillow shares one secret
It knows the stories
The ones that come at night
The secrets behind your tears

Find

And when those eyes spark
When that soul glows
From a woman finding her power

Watch your step
No, behind you
Don't fall

Look

There is beauty everywhere
You just need to know where to look
And how to slow down
To see it
And appreciate it

Little

There is so little we understand
Yet there are souls around us who do

Words You Say, Words I Know

You say I am weak
I know I am strong
You say I am crazy
I know what I believe
You say I am too sensitive
I know I am a deeply feeling person
You say get a grip
I have a tight one
You say watch my back
I always do
You say I don't know
I know you underestimate me
You say grow up
I did that a long time ago
You say I am worthless
I say think again
The words you say
Come from your heart, not mine
I know my truth
The words I know
Spark from my soul
And will not be dimmed
Will not be used to please others
Will not be taken from me
Words you say
Words I know

Floating

Escape into bliss
To be weightless
Like a bird
To be free of thought
There is no pain
Like being free
Just peace
Tranquility
You are one
Healing
Floating

Flowers

Beautiful, delicate
Timeless, vibrant
Soft, magical
But when cut
And taken from the ground
When they grow strong
They slowly fade, wilt
When the water runs out
They dry to the core
Fields of flowers
Bunches, bundles
A flower, or a single petal
Maybe women are so drawn to flowers
And look at them in awe
And understanding
Because women are much like them
And they understand
Beyond the beauty that is seen
They see what lies within
They meaning, they know
That many overlook
When looking at flowers

Tremendous

There is a tremendous hurt
Pain, suffering
When one has been hurt
Emotionally
Physically
Not acknowledged
Not seen or appreciated
But there is tremendous strength
In the fight and the will it takes
To grow and rise
It doesn't mean the scars aren't there
But the drive is
To be above, move on and ahead
It's tremendous

I'm Fine

I'm tired
Fed up
Drained
Hurt
I'm in pain
I'm sad
Good days and bad
But I'm tired
And that's okay
But
I'll reply
I'm fine

Lone Wolf

The lone wolf
Stares up at the moon
In awe and wonder
Curiosity and dreams
Yet, in such sadness
A deep, primal feeling
That cannot be escaped
The moon and stars resonate within
The majestic howl, known too well
Solid in stories and songs
Strong in spirit and soul
A fighter, a wolf
Yet the lone wolf stands
Wondering what the feeling is
Wondering why

Confuse

Don't confuse

Being lost

With being on your journey

It's all part of the process

There are many ups and downs

Successes and failures

It's all part of the growth

The change

Becoming who you are

You'll always be a work in progress

Trust yourself

Trust the process

And don't confuse

Being lost with being on your journey

Where The Road Takes Me

The wheels keep rolling
To a place where the road takes me
The sunrises and sunsets
The moon and the stars
And the glare of the midday sun
The rhythm of the road
Soon becomes its own song
Rolling hills
Waves of thunder
Mustangs running wild
Tall forests to the ocean shore
Birds dancing overhead
Waving passerby's
And the wheels keep rolling
To a place where the road takes me

Engrained

When you've been hurt
Torn, broken
Knocked to your knees
You unlearn and learn things
That change you forever
And not the good things
It changes who you are
You lose yourself
You forget how to love
You misunderstand trust
It becomes engrained
You crumble
When you're treated right
Respected, honored
Lifted from your knees
You unlearn and learn things
That change you forever
And all the good things
It changed who you are
You find yourself
You learn how to love
You understand trust
It becomes engrained
You rise

Along The Way

You'll get lost
Amongst the paths to take
You'll need to ask for the way
But take your time for breaks
Look at maps, follow your heart
Struggle up the mountains
Coast to the ocean shore
Plow through snow, brave the heat
Push on, collapse, rise, continue on
You'll get lost
In all the trials and adventures of life
But you'll always find what you need
And where you're going
Along the way

Fire

The raging fire
Ignites souls from afar
The breathing fire
Melts things together
The glow of embers
Inspire a calming rhythm
The dissipating smoke
Carries stories to distant stars
Fire brings life
Tranquility, peace
Wonder, the end of a story
To be ignited again
In a new fire another day

Clean and Keep

Darling girl –
If your mascara runs
And the tissues run low
Clean it up
If your lip gloss fades
And your lips curl to a smile
Keep that one

Did You?

Do you see?
Or blow by it as you scroll
As quickly as it appeared
Feel some sympathy
Then move on
Without a word
Do you really see?
Do you hear the cries?
Do you notice the hints?
Do you know what's going on?
Do you understand?
Do you care to ask?
It takes a second of your time
Do you see?
Or they'll blow out of this life
As quickly as they appeared
Feel some sympathy
They moved on
Without a word
Do you really see?
Did you?

Echoes

What is that echo
In the distant morning fog
It calls to me, rivers to hilltops
There's a magic in the air
That cannot be explained
A sense of being, freedom
To be discovered when ignited
As the fires blaze overhead in the sky
Only for the deep souls to see
Keys handed one by one in time
To light the way on an unseen path
A path that sparks
And forever changes the soul
Marks on the heart, until death
Always finding the way back
Nothing takes it away
What is that echo
In the distant morning fog
Echoes of dreams becoming reality
Echoes of life and love
Echoes that last an eternity
That only some will know

Impact

Words written

Travel the seas

Glass waters

And turbulent storms

To end up in the hands

Of one who needs them the most

Encouragement

Love

Understanding

To know they are seen

It makes an impact

Not just on their life

But on those lives

It touched along the way

Can't Help Who You Love

People come and go
Some you love
Or think you do
Some guide you
Show you the way
Some hurt you
Bring you to your knees
All are valuable lessons
But throughout
And within it all
The one is always there
They always come back
You know it in your heart
You can't help who you love

Never Understand

Until it happens to you
You'll never understand
So, don't claim that you do
The pain, the hurt
The raw emotions
The nightmares
Being on edge
Reminders all around
We know ourselves best
What works and what doesn't
Until it happens to you
You'll never understand
So, don't claim that you do

Strong

Even the strong ones
Break down and cry

Angels

Even Angels cry

Who You Love

When you feel it
Deep in your soul
When you know
You know without question
You can't help
Who you love

Magic

When only magic
Seals it
Into one

Your Fight

Escape your body
Cold as ice
Not even there
Until it happens to you
Forgive yourself
Then come back
Enter your body
Hot as fire
Take it all back
This is your right
Your fight

Lonely

It's a lonely feeling
To be alone
When you try
So hard
To scream it to the world
Make an impact
Share your story
Speak volumes
It's a lonely
Feeling

Exist

Where do I exist
Between the lines
Amongst the sunrises
The sunsets
The space between the stars
Within the shadows
Or in the light of the moon
Where do I exist
Amongst the herd
Or leading the pack
Riding the waves
Sitting in a stream
Or diving into depths unknown
Puling in my veins
Dancing to my heartbeat
Shaking or hyper-focused
Where do I exist
Within it all?

To Be Lonely

They say
To be alone
Is a lonely thing
I say
To be amongst many
Is a lonely thing
For only within a few
Who truly see and understand
Is where loneliness does not exist

Love Has

Love has no limits
No bounds
No restraints
No judgements
Love knows not
Of age
Of past
Of mistakes
Love is true
Love is a key
Love has your back
Watches your six
Through thick and thin
Love has no limits

Still

Behind a poker face
Screams a war in the eyes

Chance

If you give a chance to see
There is magic all around
Within the raindrops
Sparkling in the mist
The stars
The twinkling lights
If you only
Give a chance
To see

Swim Together

We will swim together, my friend
For only we know the depths
That our minds and hearts swim at
We are a tribe of one
We see each other, we understand
Because us too, me too
You are not alone, we are not alone
It will not define us
We will swim together from the depths
And come crashing in with the waves
A force to be reckoned with
I see you
Let's swim together

Forever

What's forever?
Not the material things
The replaceable
It's the irreplaceable
The perseverant things
The flowers that grow in the storm
The moon coming and going
The sunrises and sunsets
The life that blooms after a devastation
It perseveres
It remains
That's forever

Magic

Magic is
Unexpected
And all knowing
It flows and exists
Within and all around
It is not greedy
It does not hurt
It is there and it guides
Lights the way
Brings confidence
Where it was once lost
Amongst the stars
In the dust
Submerged in the waters
Dancing in the firelight
Twinkling away in the hearts
Of those
Who see
And have
The magic

Saw

I think you saw
Through the mist and haze
Against all words said
What the truth was
Of who I really am
You disregarded it all
Took it for yourself
And saw me
For who I am
As you knew
As you saw me

Invisible

Gasp
Breathe
Choose this life
Live
You are brave
Breathe

One Day

One day
They'll know
The reason
That the reason
I am alive today
Is because of them
They'll know

Tired

I'm tired
Of being hurt
Betrayed
I'm tired
Of holding back
Lying
Here I am
All of me
All I stand for
All I love
For all to see
I'm tired of hiding
Here I am
Take it as it is
Or please, go away

Another Day

It's just another day
Just like the others
It's okay, don't worry
You'll be alright

Ultimate

And so it is written
Not in stone
Not on paper
Not by oath
But by heart
And memory
With honesty
Dedication and truth
Ultimate sacrifice
Ultimate doing
To be bound
Committed
As one
That is truth
That is love
And so it is written

Trust

When a woman knows
She is trusted and respected
She gives her all.
Strong, free and wild

When a woman knows
She is controlled and monitored
She's no longer yours to keep
Lesson learned

Can't Deny

I can't deny it
This feeling
It comes around
Once in a lifetime
You think you know
Then you're hurt and betrayed
You give up hope
Until the one comes along
And then you know
And you can't deny

A Thousand

There are a thousand reasons
That cannot be explained by words
They are gained
When given the keys
To be known and understood
There are a thousand reasons
Why it prevails
Why it means so much
Why it makes you feel free
It's surreal and full of magic
There are a thousand reasons
Why
I love you

Infinite

There are a thousand reasons why
And even that isn't enough
It is a feeling
A magic that only we hold and know
The world will never know what hit it
Starting with one foggy morning
To ignite and bond
And move mountains with earthquakes
The power of those songs
Always brought us back together
Why?
Because even when words can't explain
The love is there to stay
My moon and my stars
I am yours and you are mine
To run under the stars
Against the wind
To swim the deepest waters
And brace the fires
There are a thousand reasons
Why
I love you
There are a thousand reasons
Why
I want to spend my life with you

Can She?

She can

Can she?

Never say it again

Despite it all

Can she

In her heart

But

Does she know?

When she falls

It's a strong word

Never

If she can

She doesn't know

Maybe she never will

Never

Read that backwards. Because – She Can

Treat Her Right

No woman
Should be treated
With disrespect
Ignorance
Never to be gaslighted
As a convenience
As a slave to daily tasks
Talked to like a wall
Taken for granted
Underestimated
Never
No woman should be treated
As such
True men treat women
Like Goddesses , Angels, Warriors
With the upmost respect
Admiration
Passion and love
Because when that happens
It is given in return
Watch that woman
Treat her right
See her fly
Disrespect her
See the power of those wings
Treat her right

Genuine

There is one smile
That should only be worn
By a woman

A genuine one

Never Knew

I never knew
The word hate
Until I found it
And learned
That hate could go deeper
Than the depths of hell

Saved

You saved me
All that matters
Is the story we know
The truth we live
You saved me
I saved myself
All that matters
Is the story I know
The truth I live
I saved myself
All that matters
Is my heart, soul, and spirit
Are free
I am saved
We are saved
All of us

Eve

The night before
Everything is so quiet
And still
The looming magic in the air
The logs crack and spark
The lights twinkle
Inside and out
Jackets are hung
Smiles abound
The windows begin to frost
The stars align
And prepare for the day ahead
It is the eve
Full of magic
Where memories are made
And told for years to come

You Thought

All this time you thought
I was naïve; young
Weak, unknowing
That I would break
And I would fall for your lies
Your pain and chains
You thought
You could bring me to my knees
Do what you wanted
To please yourself and get away with it
Let me tell you this
All this time you thought that –
In truth I was wiser than my years
Strong, knowing
I would never break
I would rise, I would stand
Despite the pain and chains
You thought you'd bring me to my knees?
Haha, no
I'll bring you to yours
To never do what you did again to any woman
To never get away with it again
Let me tell you this
Cowards and fools
Abusers never get away with it
If not on paper, never in soul
All this time you thought you could

You have no say

No power

No right

You have nothing

Who is on their knees now?

Let Them Fly

Let them fly, mama
Let them fly
It's not easy
Standing back
Letting them grow
Letting them be challenged
Releasing your grasp
So they can find their own
It's not easy mama
I know, trust me
But, we have to spread our wings
So they can spread theirs
Let them fly, mama
Let them fly

What It's Worth

For what it's worth
It doesn't matter
What others think
Just what you know
What you've seen
Been through
For what it's worth
Those close to you
Will know
It doesn't matter
What the others think
Just what you know
For what it's worth

New Year, New Day

'tis not the end
It's another new day
A new start
A time to reflect and be
To continue those steps forward
To conquer those dreams
Follow your heart
Tackle obstacles in your way
To continue your journey
For who you are meant to be
And where you're meant to go
Trust the process
Enjoy the journey
And remember
'tis not the end
It's another new day

Happy New Year

Count Your Tears

Only you, my dear
Can count your tears
When the lights go out
When nobody else knows
Only you
Can count how many
And know

Another Day

It's just another day
Just like the others
It's okay, don't worry
You'll be alright

Tired

I'm tired
Of being hurt
Betrayed
I'm tired
Of holding back
Here I am
All of me
All I stand for
All I love
For all to see
I'm tired of hiding
Here I am
Take it as it is
Or please, go away

One Day

One day
They'll know
The reason
That the reason
I am alive today
Is because of them
They'll know

Invisible

Gasp
Breathe
Choose this life
Live
You are brave
Breathe

Saw

I think you saw
Through the mist and the haze
Against all words said
What the truth was
Of who I really am
You disregarded it all
Took it for yourself
And saw me
For who I am
As you knew
As you saw me

Hanna

It's sad, but true
You put a bag on to block out the world
At the end of days
Took your last breaths
I respect and understand your choice
But I wish it weren't so
You were not only mine
But a friend of many
Your cat, a friend as well
One just like him lives with me now
You lived a full life
You were a beautiful person
But you saw the depths of hell
In those camps
People taken from you
Mistreated
Camps that make lips tremble
When spoken
But you carried on
Hanna- I'll always remember your name
And how special you were to me
And many others
You live in my heart, always
And my cat, just like yours, same name
Max
I miss you, dearly
Hanna

Follow

I'll always strive
For better
Set goals
Achieve them
Do whatever it takes
To set my soul on fire
I'll follow my heart
Even if it means
Taking the less traveled path
I'll listen
Take the keys
Follow the way
Trust the journey

Feel

What a thing it is
To think you know love
And feel nothing at all

But wait –

What a thing it is
To truly know love
And feel everything in one

That's Okay

I'm scared
I'm falling
And, that's okay
When we share our weaknesses
People love it
Not to see our suffering
But to know they're not alone
You're not alone
We are all scared
We all fall
But, we all
Can find a way
And, that's okay

Comes And Goes

It comes and it goes
Like the rising tides
Some days you know
Some days it hides
You trust and you break
You pour it all in
You wonder if it's fake
You question, wonder, breathe
You know when you should
And when you shouldn't leave
It's hard to know
Like the rising tides
When to come and when to go
Take the time you need
And you'll know

It's Okay, Mama

I love that you share
Yourself at your weakest
When you're mad
When you're sad and ashamed
When you question
When you fall
I don't love it because you're struggling
No
I love it because
It's the same for me
We're both going through that
Both having a bad day, moment
Questioning, wondering
Both feeling like we're falling apart
And failing
But we recognize it, we share it
So many others relate
We're all in this together
And we're okay
We're okay

When I Need Time

Please understand
When I need to breathe
When I need to absorb
Process, and be
When I need time
Please be patient
Please understand
When I need time

Secret

Keep your secret
It's okay
I already know
I already saw
Little do you think you know
I smell lies a mile away
And I knew, I know
I saw, I see
It's not hard
But don't worry
I've heard
Karma does her fair share

Heavy

When everything
Is on your shoulders
Expected to do it all
Get it all done
The burden
The drain
The effect
It gets heavy
Too heavy
To carry
Watch
What effect
It will have
In the end

Thank You

Thank you
For being there
For being a friend
For helping me
When I needed it
And when I didn't say I did
Thank you
For knowing
For seeing
For being
Thank you

Finding

Finding answers
Falling into my own
Understanding
Unraveling
Being
Letting go
To find
Me
Amongst the mess
To find my smile
A start of a new story
Finding my soul
My heart
I'm finding
Me

Help

It's hard to ask
For help when we need it
It's hard to recognize
When it is we need to ask
But right now
I rise above it all
I never have had to before
And right now
I'm asking for help
Please help
Please
Help

Bell

I see you, mama
Your head in your hands
Crying
Defeated
Stressed
Tired
Trying to be perfect
To be everything
I see you
I also see
You wiping your tears
A minute before the bell rings
To put on a smile
For your child
To hide all that goes on
Behind the mask
Take your time mama
Before the bell rings
Do what you need to do
I see you
I'm there too

Just So…

Just so you know
I notice
Just so you know
I see you
Just so you know
I care
The spoken
The unspoken
The seen
The unseen
I know
I understand
Just so you know
You're not alone

Demons In Dreams

The things of nightmares
We wish for dreams of flying
Instead, when our inner turmoil
Sends us messages
Our dreams haunt us
Vivid, detailed
You can see, smell, feel everything
But, these are the dreams
That are inescapable
Of things no human should endure
Or face or see
The terrors
The sadness
The pain
The fear
When these terrors come about
Find the meaning, the reason why
There is always a sign, an explanation
There are demons in dreams
It's up to you to find out why
And conquer them
So you can, once again, fly

Can't Find

I can't find the words
To explain what I feel
When emotions run high
My body, a nonstop rush
It's hard to pinpoint
Hard to find
Deep down, I know
But right now, I can't find them

Valid

It's valid what you think
The things you question
What you wonder about
That's normal, it's okay
It's healthy
It's valid

Collide

At some point
We all collide
Our stories
Our lives
Mesh into one
The people you walk by
Aren't just anybody, or nobody
They are in your life
They impact it
We just don't notice
Until the time comes to see
And feel
We all
Collide

Made It

This is about a girl
A girl who made it, in the end
Despite all the crushing words
Blows to her body
Abuse to mind and soul
Tears at her heart
Collapsing at her feet
Wondering if she'd make it
In fact, she did
She made it
That was about a girl
This is about a woman
A woman who made it, in the end

Okay?

How are you?

I'm fine.

Are you okay?

Well, here's the thing…

Behind the mask
And poker faces
Behind the artificial smiles
Fake replies
How am I?
Not great
Are you okay?
Not really
I know and believe
I will be one day
But, right now I'm not
But
What do I say?

Reply

How do I reply?
Say I'm good, and you walk away
Say I'm fine, and you carry on
How do I reply?
Things are good, and you mind your own
Say it's all fine, and you move along

Truth is
I'm good, but I really am not
I'm here, but am not
I'm fine, but I really am not
I'm handling life, but am not

Truth is
Things are good, but they're also bad
I don't know what to say
Things are fine, but could be much better
So, how do I reply?

Take The Pain

It's the only thing I know
And I wish it weren't so
This nonstop pain
Drains every part of me
Please, take the pain
Toss it off a ledge
Put it to the fire
Throw it to the wind
Shelter my soul
It's the only thing I know
And I want to be free
Of this pain
Please
Take the pain away

Break

When you bend
Do you break?
When you're pushed
Do you fall?
When you're drowning
Amongst it all
How many times
Must it take
To bring you to your knees
Or even worse
To your grave
Before ones eyes open
To see the real reason
That you're breaking
Before you truly
And finally
Break?

Who Knew?

That's what it feels like
Who knew?
The real break
You never saw coming
The real break
That ripped your core
There's no coming back from that
Who knew?

She Is A Mountain

She cannot be moved
Curves that go beyond view
Braves the elements
House the wild things
Sings to the moon
And dances in the sunlight
Many trek the paths
Not all make it to the top
Some twist and turn
Some are an easy route
But watch for the sticks and stones
Avalanches and rivers
Leave the wolves
They'll keep their eyes on you
Protecting her spirit
She puts up with it all
And stands her ground
She is a mountain

Thank You

Joanna
A Flutter In The Stars

Made in the USA
Las Vegas, NV
10 June 2021